1|15

···A **TIMELINE HISTORY** OF THE···

THIRTEEN COLONIES

···**TIMELINE TRACKERS**: AMERICA'S BEGINNINGS···

MARY K. PRATT

Lerner Publications Company
Minneapolis

CONTENTS

Lerner Publications Company
A division of Lerner Publishing Group, Inc.
241 First Avenue North
Minneapolis, MN 55401 USA

For reading levels and more information, look up this title at www.lernerbooks.com.

Library of Congress Cataloging-in-Publication Data

Pratt, Mary K.
   A timeline history of the thirteen colonies / by Mary Pratt.
      pages   cm
   Includes index.
   ISBN 978–1–4677–3639–8 (lib. bdg. : alk. paper)
   ISBN 978–1–4677–4754–7 (eBook)
   1. United States—History—Colonial period, ca. 1600–1775—Chronology—Juvenile literature.
I. Title.
E188.P73 2015
973.2—dc23   2013041250

Manufactured in the United States of America
1 – BP – 7/15/14

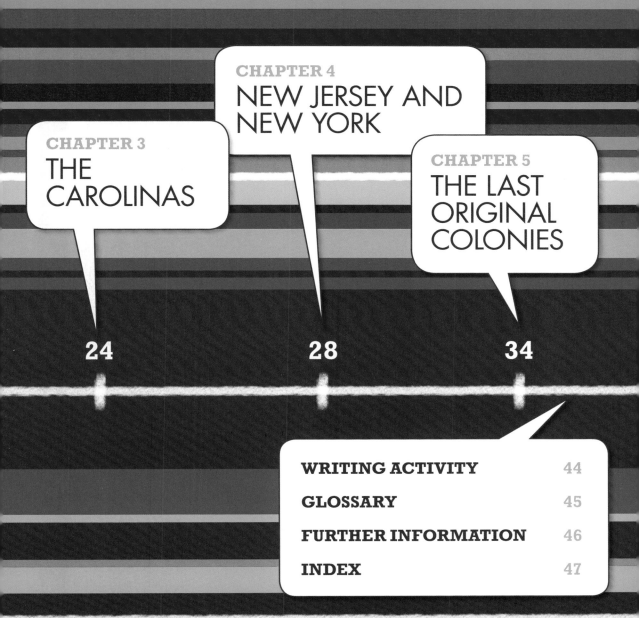

COVER PHOTO:
Map from 1784 by cartographer F. L. Güssefeld, depicting the colonies
that were the forerunners of the present-day United States

INTRODUCTION

In the 1500s and the 1600s, Europeans thought of the Americas as a strange and exotic land. They called it the New World, and the bravest of them set out to colonize it. The Spanish preferred Central and South America for the warmer weather and gold. The French settled in Canada because it had more of the valuable furs they wanted.

That left the eastern shores of the modern-day United States available to England. Like other European settlers, the English thought of the New World as unclaimed land. Few of them had any knowledge or understanding of the American Indians who lived there.

Some English settlers came to the New World to make money. They grew valuable crops and took advantage of the land's natural resources. Others, such as the Puritans, came to establish new religious communities. They were looking to practice their beliefs freely. Still others, such as the Quakers, came for a different reason. They hoped to build a fairer community than the one they left behind in England.

Regardless of the reasons they came, the settlers encountered many challenges. Early settlers found the work of establishing a colony hard. They also discovered that their attitudes toward the American Indians created many conflicts. The settlers suffered hunger and disease and death.

Yet these hardships and high rates of death did not stop the flow of new colonists. Over time, more and more settlers came from England and other European nations. Together, they colonized the land that would become America.

TIMELINES

In this book, a series of dates and important events appear in timelines. Timelines are a graphic way of showing a sequence of events over a specific time period. A timeline often reveals the cause and effect of events. It can help to explain how one happening in history leads to the next. The timelines in this book display important turning points in the early history of each of the original thirteen colonies. Solid lines in the timelines indicate regular intervals of time. Dashed lines represent bigger jumps in time.

CHAPTER 1

The EARLIEST COLONIES

In the early 1600s, the king of England began giving settlers permission to colonize the New World. The permission came in the form of a charter. This document stated who could start the colony and who would govern it.

There were two main types of charters. A royal charter meant the colony belonged to the king. He would appoint governors and sometimes a council to govern it. The second kind of charter was a proprietary charter. It gave private individuals the power to control the colony. These men were usually wealthy citizens who remained in England. They wanted to make money by sending settlers to work in their colonies. They paid for the supplies to start a new colony. But they also got much of the colony's profits. The colonists harvested crops and other natural resources, such as timber and fur. They then shipped those valuable goods back to England and other European countries to be sold.

1606: London businessmen establish Virginia.

1608–1609: Captain John Smith is in command of Jamestown.

1609: Fights break out between the colonists and nearby American Indian tribes.

VIRGINIA

| 1606 | 1607 | 1608 | 1609 | 1610 | 1611 |

1607: Settlers establish Jamestown.

Nov. 1608: A powerful Pamunkey chief named Powhatan stops trading with the colonists.

Virginia

The first colony that the English successfully settled was Virginia. In 1606 King James I gave a group of wealthy investors permission to colonize the territory. This group of businessmen was known as the Virginia Company. The company sent settlers across the Atlantic Ocean. Those settlers reached the Chesapeake Bay in early 1607. They built wooden shelters and a fort. They named their settlement Jamestown, after King James.

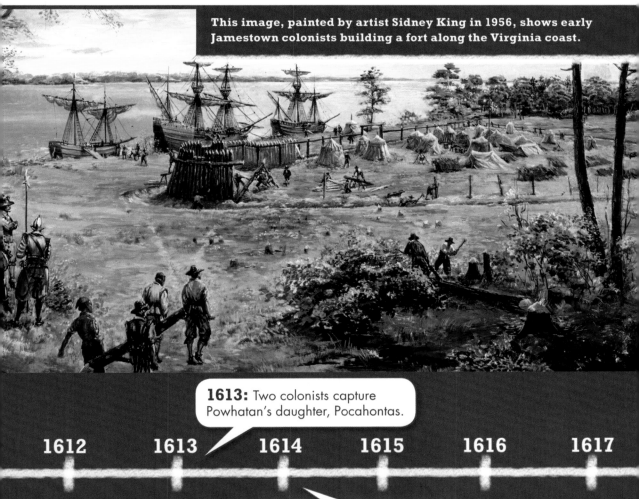

This image, painted by artist Sidney King in 1956, shows early Jamestown colonists building a fort along the Virginia coast.

1613: Two colonists capture Powhatan's daughter, Pocahontas.

1612   1613   1614   1615   1616   1617

1607–1622: The Virginia Company sends ten thousand more settlers. But only 20 percent of them are still alive by 1622.

1614: Fighting between the colonists and American Indians ends when Pocahontas marries an Englishman named John Rolfe.

Life was harsh for the settlers from the moment they arrived. They had little food and depended on the help of local American Indians. At first, the Pamunkey American Indians welcomed the newcomers and even shared their food. But they soon resented the settlers who were taking over their land. They stopped helping the settlers, and some of those settlers starved. Many also became sick from diseases. Of the 104 settlers, 66 died in the first year.

Even so, the Virginia Company sent over more settlers. It assigned the colony a leader named Captain John Smith.

Captain John Smith

Smith forced the colonists to farm for six hours every day. That way, they could grow enough food to stay alive. By about 1614, the settlers were also growing tobacco. It soon became a profitable crop for the colony. But the Virginia Company spent more money settling the colony than the company made selling goods. In 1624 the company ran out of money, and the king took over the colony.

Around this time, Virginia colonists began using slaves from Africa. These men, women, and children were often brought

1619: The first African slaves arrive in Jamestown.

1618   1619   1620   1621   1622   1623

1622: On March 22, the Pamunkey American Indians kill 347 settlers in an attack.

from Africa against their will. They worked the farmland without pay.

Meanwhile, the tense relationship with the area's American Indians worsened. The two sides launched deadly attacks throughout colonial times. Yet despite many difficulties, the colony grew. By the mid-1700s, Virginia contained one-fifth of the thirteen colonies' total population.

EARLY SLAVERY

The first slaves in the colonies were American Indians. They were soon joined by African slaves who first arrived in the American colonies in 1619. But the Africans did not remain slaves their entire lives. They worked without pay for a fixed amount of time. Then they were freed. That system began to change in the mid-1600s. New colonial laws made it legal to treat African slaves like property. Owners could keep Africans in slavery for their entire lives.

Colonist Nathaniel Bacon disagreed with how Jamestown's leaders were handling relations with American Indians. He and his supporters burned Jamestown in protest in 1676.

1625: On May 13, King Charles I proclaims Virginia a royal colony.

1644: On April 18, another surprise attack kills more than four hundred settlers.

1624   1625   1650   1675   1700

1624: The Virginia Company runs out of money.

1676: Nathaniel Bacon leads Bacon's Rebellion with the goal of killing every American Indian in Virginia.

1705: Virginia's lawmakers begin passing many laws to limit the rights of slaves and free blacks.

Massachusetts

In 1620 a group of people from England boarded a ship called the *Mayflower*. Many of them were Christians known as Puritans. Puritans disagreed with the beliefs and practices of the Church of England, or Anglican Church. At the time, everyone in England was required to practice the Anglican religion. Those who followed other forms of Christianity were badly mistreated.

The Puritans on the *Mayflower* hoped to escape that mistreatment. They planned to form a community based on their own religious beliefs. This group of Puritans came to be known as the Pilgrims. They were heading for the Virginia territory. But on November 11, 1620, the *Mayflower* landed in modern-day Massachusetts. The Pilgrims soon established the community of Plymouth, Massachusetts.

The Pilgrims depended on nearby Wampanoag American Indians for food and advice. Yet they did not respect the American Indians or their beliefs. The peaceful relationship between the two sides quickly fell apart.

Other Puritan settlers followed the Pilgrims to Massachusetts in the early to mid-1600s. These new settlers established other communities based on their strict religious faith. These communities were not always very peaceful.

MASSACHUSETTS

1614: Captain John Smith explores the New England coast.

Nov.11, 1620: The *Mayflower* lands on Cape Cod. The Mayflower Compact is signed.

April 1621: The Pilgrims sign a peace treaty with Wampanoag chief Massasoit.

1612   1614   1616   1618   1620   1622

Dec. 1620: The *Mayflower* lands in Plymouth.

Oct. 1621: The Pilgrims share a feast of thanksgiving with Massasoit and other American Indians.

Throughout the 1600s, Massachusetts settlers battled American Indians. The colonists also did not practice religious tolerance. Instead, they threw out settlers who had different opinions or religious beliefs. Some of those banished settlers went on to establish other colonies.

Pilgrims in England prepare to board the *Mayflower* at the start of their journey to the New World. Their travels would end four months later on the shores of Massachusetts.

1624   1626   1628   1630   1632   1634

1630: The Massachusetts Bay Company is formed. It sets up a democratic government.

From the time the first colonists arrived in Massachusetts, they worked to set up a new government. Puritan men elected their leaders, including a governor and a legislature. This system helped establish the idea of a free democracy in the English colonies. But Massachusetts, like the other English colonies, did not extend such freedom to others.

In the 1690s, people accused of witchcraft in Salem, Massachusetts, faced trial. In this illustration from 1876, seventeen-year-old Mary Walcott is accused in court.

1641: The Puritans pass the first law in the colonies to make slavery legal.

1675: A deadly war against American Indians known as King Philip's War begins.

1636   1638   1640   1674   1676   1678   1684

1651: Massachusetts claims control over Maine.

1676: King Philip's War ends in August.

In 1641 the colony was the first to make slavery legal. It also continued to mistreat people who practiced other religions. Such a strict society led to a deadly event known as the Salem witch trials. In the 1690s, nearly two hundred people were falsely accused of practicing witchcraft. The accusations began in the town of Salem Village. About twenty-four people were found guilty and hanged. The trials ended only after a group of Massachusetts leaders put a stop to them.

The colony continued to face other challenges as it grew. A flow of colonists set up more and more towns and cities. The colonists often battled with local American Indians over the land.

The colony's government also underwent changes. In the late 1600s, the king of England tried to take more control of the colony. He wanted to take away the right of the colonists to choose their own governor. The colonists fought against this control. But they struggled throughout colonial times over how much power the king should have.

PASSENGERS ON THE *MAYFLOWER*

The Puritans were not the only ones to journey aboard the *Mayflower*. They shared the voyage with another group of settlers. The group included merchants and laborers. On November 11, 1620, the two groups on board the ship signed the Mayflower Compact. This document helped establish the first government in Plymouth.

1692: The Salem witch trials begin.

1686   1688   1690   1692   1694   1702   1704

1693: The Salem witch trials end.

1704: The French and American Indians attack and kill colonists in the western part of the colony.

New Hampshire

The English began settling in New Hampshire in the early 1620s. By the 1630s, it became known as a land of freedom for people like the Reverend John Wheelwright. Wheelwright lived in Massachusetts. His religious ideas differed from those of the strict Puritans. Massachusetts leaders threw him and his followers out of Massachusetts in late 1637. Wheelwright established a settlement in New Hampshire called Exeter in 1638. Other settlers from Massachusetts soon followed.

New Hampshire did not remain independent for long. In 1641 four small settlements agreed to be governed by Massachusetts. By 1643 Exeter had also agreed to become part of Massachusetts. The two colonies would remain united until 1680. Then New Hampshire became a separate royal colony.

The colony's status changed again six years later. In 1686 King James II formed one large colony called the Dominion of New England. It included modern-day Maine, New Hampshire, Vermont, Massachusetts, Rhode Island,

John Wheelwright

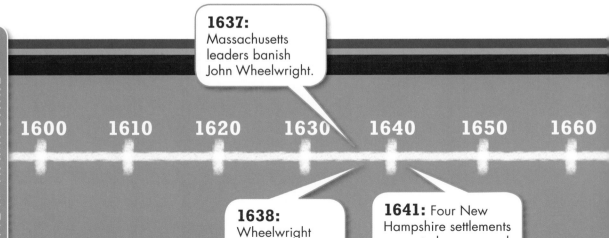

1637: Massachusetts leaders banish John Wheelwright.

1600   1610   1620   1630   1640   1650   1660

1638: Wheelwright and his followers establish Exeter.

1641: Four New Hampshire settlements agree to be governed by the Massachusetts Bay Colony.

Connecticut, New York, and New Jersey. The king appointed a single, powerful governor. Colonists in New Hampshire and elsewhere protested this change. They thought the king and his governor had too much power over them. They even jailed the governor. After three years, the Dominion of New England collapsed. Soon after, New Hampshire once again became its own colony.

This illustration shows New Hampshire in 1680, the year it became an independent colony.

1680: New Hampshire becomes a separate colony on September 18.

1689: The Pennacook tribe leads surprise attacks on New Hampshire settlers. The Dominion of New England is ended after colonists protest.

1670   1680   1690   1700   1710   1720

1686: King James II creates the Dominion of New England.

1690: The colony's non-American Indian population reaches four thousand.

1713: American Indians known as the Eastern Indians sign the Treaty of Portsmouth with the colonists.

CHAPTER 2
The NEXT COLONIES

The Puritans were not the only ones seeking religious freedom in the New World. Other Christians in England also struggled to practice their religions freely. They too came to America hoping for a fresh start. Some of these freedom seekers settled colonies such as Maryland and Rhode Island. But they differed from the Puritans. They not only wanted to practice their own religion freely. They also tried to be accepting of other religious beliefs.

Maryland

In 1632 King Charles I granted a man named Cecilius Calvert 12 million acres (4.8 million hectares) of land just north of Virginia. Calvert was also known as Lord Baltimore. He owned and governed Maryland, and he wanted to make money off the colony. But he also wanted the colony to welcome Catholics like himself.

MARYLAND

1631: The English establish a trading post on Kent Island off of Maryland.

1634: Cecilius Calvert's brother, Leonard Calvert, becomes governor of Maryland.

| 1630 | 1632 | 1634 | 1636 | 1638 | 1640 |

1632: King Charles I grants Maryland to Cecilius Calvert, or Lord Baltimore.

1635: Maryland and Virginia battle over ownership of Kent Island.

1638: Maryland takes ownership of Kent Island.

Catholics were not well-treated by Protestants in England. In Maryland, Lord Baltimore hoped Catholics and Protestants could live together in peace. To his disappointment, not many Catholics moved to Maryland. Most of the settlers were Protestant.

Lord Baltimore wanted to attract more settlers. He developed a generous new plan. He granted 100 acres (40 hectares) for every adult who came to Maryland. He gave away another 50 acres (20 hectares) for every child under sixteen who came along. The bigger the family, the more land the family received.

Van Sweringen's Inn was built in the mid-1600s in St. Mary's City, Maryland. It has been restored so visitors can see what the colony's original structures looked like.

mid-1600s: The colony grants free land to new settlers.

1642   1644   1646   1648   1650

1649: The Religious Toleration Act protects religious freedom.

Lord Baltimore's land policy brought experienced farmers to Maryland. Those farmers became wealthy by growing valuable tobacco. As a result, Maryland continued to grow and thrive. Meanwhile, the colony was becoming more dependent on the work of African slaves. It relied on them to work in the fields and in homes.

As the colony prospered, it continued to accept different religious beliefs. The colony's lawmaking body was called the

Visitors to the Godiah Spray Tobacco Plantation, a living history museum in Maryland, can see how tobacco would have been harvested in the 1600s.

1654: The Maryland General Assembly rejects the Religious Toleration Act.

1654   1656   1658   1660   1662   1664

1663: The colony makes slavery legal.

Maryland General Assembly. In 1649 the assembly passed a law called the Religious Toleration Act. The law said that settlers had the right to practice their own religions freely.

That right was short-lived. The lawmakers in the Maryland General Assembly put an end to the Religious Toleration Act in 1654. After that, religious acceptance declined. By the late 1600s, Protestants and Catholics were fighting over power in the colony.

Colonists in Maryland also had a difficult time respecting their American Indian neighbors. Many American Indians had fled the colony after English settlers first took over. Those who remained feared that the colonists would control more and more of their land. Such fears eventually led to American Indian attacks against Maryland colonists. Even so, Maryland continued to be a thriving colony.

CONVICTS IN THE COLONIES

Between 1718 and 1775, Great Britain sent about fifty thousand convicts to the colonies. Each of these people had been found guilty of a crime. They were mostly young, unmarried men who did not have a trade or a skill. Most ended up in Maryland and Virginia. Convicts often found work on farms. Even so, many colonists were angry that England was sending criminals to their communities.

1718: Great Britain begins sending criminals to Maryland.

1692: Maryland becomes a royal colony.

| 1692 | 1694 | 1696 | 1698 | 1700 | 1750 |

ca. 1697–1707: The Nanticoke and Conoy people flee Maryland.

1750: Black slaves make up about 40 percent of Maryland's population.

Connecticut

Settlers began to arrive in Connecticut in the 1630s. Some of these early colonists came from Massachusetts. Like the Puritans, they wanted to build a community that matched their religious ideals. One of those colonists was the Reverend Thomas Hooker. He and his religious followers established what became known as Hartford. It also became the colony's capital.

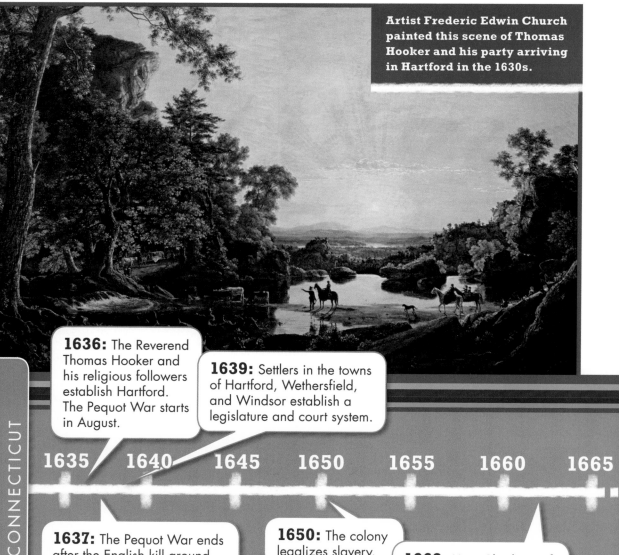

Artist Frederic Edwin Church painted this scene of Thomas Hooker and his party arriving in Hartford in the 1630s.

1636: The Reverend Thomas Hooker and his religious followers establish Hartford. The Pequot War starts in August.

1639: Settlers in the towns of Hartford, Wethersfield, and Windsor establish a legislature and court system.

1637: The Pequot War ends after the English kill around 40 percent of the Pequots' two thousand men, women, and children.

1650: The colony legalizes slavery.

1662: King Charles II of England gives Connecticut a charter that keeps the colony's right of self-government.

1635   1640   1645   1650   1655   1660   1665

Other Connecticut colonists came to earn money. Connecticut had fertile land for farming. It also had a valuable fur trade. Connecticut colonists tried to maintain peaceful relations with the local American Indian community. But that did not last long. Colonists took over American Indian lands. They also brought diseases that killed many American Indians. In response, some American Indian communities attacked English settlements. Others sided with the colonists. In 1636 the Narragansett and Mohegan American Indians joined the English in a battle against the Pequots. This became known as the Pequot War.

The colony continued to grow throughout the 1600s and the 1700s. As it grew, it established the right of the people to govern themselves. That meant the people could elect their own local leaders and lawmakers. This idea later became the foundation of the United States.

Colonists attack a Pequot fort during the Pequot War.

1689: The right to self-govern is restored when the Dominion of New England ends.

1685   1690   1695   1700   1705   1710

1687: Connecticut loses its rights to self-govern when it becomes part of the Dominion of New England.

1701: Lawmakers establish the Collegiate School, later known as Yale University.

Rhode Island

The colony of Rhode Island got its start in the early 1630s. It soon became known as a place of religious freedom. The colony's first leader was a minister from Salem, Massachusetts, named Roger Williams. In the 1630s, Williams upset religious leaders in Massachusetts. He complained that the Puritans had not done enough to separate themselves from the Church of England. The colony's leaders wanted to arrest Williams. But he escaped to the land that became Rhode Island. There he and his followers started the settlement of Providence.

A woman named Anne Hutchinson also ran into trouble in Massachusetts. She had been leading prayer meetings in her Boston home. The colony's leaders did not like Hutchinson's ideas. They banished her from Massachusetts

This statue of Roger Williams stands in Providence, Rhode Island.

1630: English and other European settlers set up trading posts and settlements in Rhode Island.

Oct. 1635: Puritan leaders in Massachusetts banish Roger Williams.

1637: Anne Hutchinson is forced out of Massachusetts.

1640: Colonists set up a government that separates church and state.

| 1630 | 1635 | 1636 | 1637 | 1638 | 1639 | 1640 |

1635: The colony establishes religious freedom.

1636: Williams buys land in June from the Narragansett American Indians and establishes the settlement of Providence.

1638: Hutchinson and her followers flee to Rhode Island.

in 1637. Hutchinson and some of her supporters fled to Rhode Island. Once there, they established the towns of Portsmouth, Newport, and Warwick.

From those early days, the colony's leaders agreed to tolerate different religious views. They also established the idea that religion and the government should be separate. This became known as separation of church and state. As a result, Rhode Island did not experience the fighting over religion that occurred in other colonies. During colonial times, the colony's farms and its fishing and sailing trades grew. As a result, Rhode Island prospered.

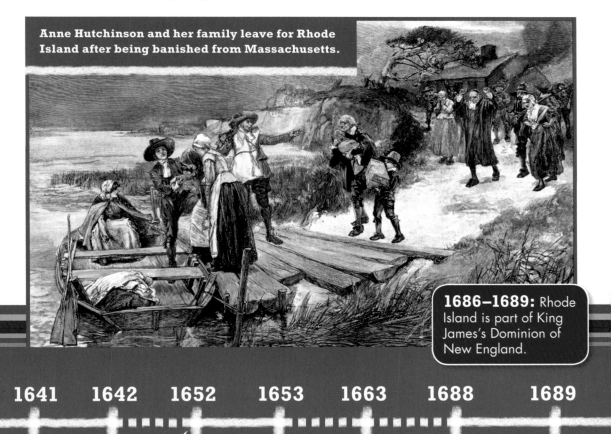

Anne Hutchinson and her family leave for Rhode Island after being banished from Massachusetts.

1686–1689: Rhode Island is part of King James's Dominion of New England.

1641   1642   1652   1653   1663   1688   1689

1652: Rhode Island makes it illegal for anyone to be enslaved for more than ten years or after the age of twenty-four.

1663: On July 18, King Charles II of England grants Rhode Island a royal charter that supports religious freedom.

CHAPTER 3

The CAROLINAS

English settlers first arrived in the Carolinas in the 1580s. They tried to establish a colony on Roanoke Island off the coast of North Carolina. The settlement failed, but settlers were still drawn to the area. By the mid-1600s, some began coming to the Carolinas from Virginia. Others sailed from the West Indies in the Caribbean Sea.

North Carolina

North Carolina was established along with South Carolina in 1663. At the time, the Carolinas were considered one large territory. King Charles II gave control of the territory to the governor of Virginia and seven Englishmen.

The Carolinas attracted settlers with promises of land. Many of these settlers created large farms called plantations. The settlers brought African slaves to work on the plantations. The slaves taught planters how to grow rice. This became an important crop in the 1690s. The plantation owners relied

1585: The first attempt to colonize the area with a settlement at Roanoke is unsuccessful.

1663: Charles II establishes a charter for the Carolinas.

NORTH CAROLINA

| 1580 | 1590 | 1600 | 1660 | 1670 | 1680 | 1690 |

1587: The second attempt to colonize the island fails.

1663–1668: Settlers from Virginia and the Caribbean colonize the coast.

1690s: Rice becomes a staple crop.

heavily on African slaves. Yet many planters treated their slaves cruelly.

These rich plantation owners also insisted on participating in the colony's government. The colony's leaders thought these colonists were too powerful. They wanted to split them up and weaken their power. So they divided the territory into North Carolina and South Carolina. North Carolina finally became its own colony in 1712.

THE LOST COLONY

The failed colony at Roanoke is sometimes called the Lost Colony. In 1587 an English ship dropped off a group of about 120 settlers on Roanoke. But the settlers were not welcomed by the American Indians who lived there. What happened next remains a mystery. English ships were unable to return to the colony until 1590. By then all the colonists had vanished. No one knows for sure what happened to them. The rescuers found the mysterious word *Croatoan* carved in wood *(below)*.

1711: The Tuscarora War against the Tuscarora tribe begins in the Carolinas.

1713: The Tuscarora War ends.

1717: The Yamasee War ends.

1700   1710   1720   1730   1740   1750

1712: North Carolina and South Carolina become separate colonies.

1715: The Yamasee and Muskogees attack settlers after being mistreated, and the Yamasee War begins.

1740s: Settlers move away from the coast into the colony's interior.

South Carolina

From their earliest days as colonists, the people of South Carolina wished to rule themselves. Wealthy plantation owners created the colony's capital city in the late 1600s. They named it Charles Towne after King Charles II. It later became known as Charleston. South Carolina's government in Charleston made sure the colony's laws reflected the beliefs of its leaders. In 1702 they passed a law that made the Church of England the colony's official religion.

In the 1720s, South Carolina became a royal colony. The colonists continued to elect their lawmakers. But the king began appointing the colony's governor. He also provided the colony with better protection from its enemies. Nearby Spanish colonists and American Indians such as the Tuscarora and Yamasee often attacked English colonists.

King Charles II

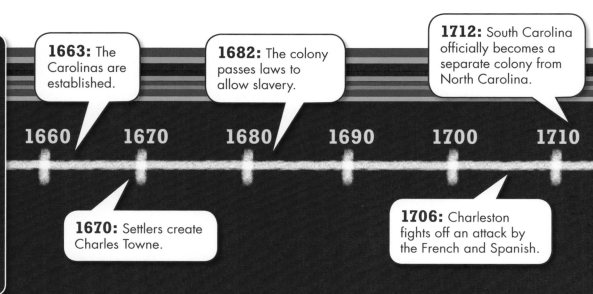

1663: The Carolinas are established.

1682: The colony passes laws to allow slavery.

1712: South Carolina officially becomes a separate colony from North Carolina.

1660 1670 1680 1690 1700 1710

1670: Settlers create Charles Towne.

1706: Charleston fights off an attack by the French and Spanish.

Like North Carolina, South Carolina had a large slave population. During the 1670s and the 1680s, slaves made up one-fourth of the Carolina population. Africans made up most of the slave population. But captured American Indians were also enslaved. Although slavery was legal in the colony, some slaves fought back. They attacked white colonists and planned rebellions. The white colonists feared a widespread slave revolt. They passed laws that made it legal to harshly control and punish their slaves.

TO BE SOLD on board the Ship Bance-Island, on tuesday the 6th of May next, at Ashley-Ferry; a choice cargo of about 250 fine healthy NEGROES, just arrived from the Windward & Rice Coast. —The utmost care has already been taken, and shall be continued, to keep them free from the least danger of being infected with the SMALL-POX, no boat having been on board, and all other communication with people from Charles-Town prevented.

Austin, Laurens, & Appleby.

N. B. Full one Half of the above Negroes have had the SMALL-POX in their own Country.

An advertisement from a newspaper announces the sale of newly arrived slaves off the coast of Charleston, South Carolina.

1720: Colonists execute slave leaders planning a rebellion.

1720   1730   1740   1750   1760   1770

1729: South Carolina becomes a royal colony.

1739: Slaves in the colony launch a fight for their freedom but are defeated.

CHAPTER 4

NEW JERSEY and NEW YORK

Like the Carolinas, the colonies of New York and New Jersey have a shared history. In the 1600s, they were part of a Dutch colony called New Netherland. Tensions ran high between the English and the Dutch. They fought over control of the slave trade and other trading. They also disagreed about who had true claim to New Netherland.

New York

In 1664 King Charles II declared that New Netherland belonged to England. He gave the large territory to his brother James, the Duke of York. The colony of New York was named after him. The land he controlled included New York, as well as New Jersey and Delaware. Later that year, England sent warships to conquer the Dutch in New Netherland. The Dutch settlers surrendered without a fight on August 27.

The English colonists in the region legalized slavery that year. They also started trading with the Five Nations of

NEW YORK

1615   1620   1625   1630   1635   1640

1624: Dutch and other European settlers arrive in New Netherland.

the Iroquois. This union of American Indians included five separate tribes. In the 1670s, the leaders of New York asked the American Indians to join them in battling enemy tribes. The conflict became known as King Philips' War.

The colonists did not return the favor to the Five Nations. In the 1680s, the French attacked the Iroquois, one of the tribes of the Five Nations. Yet the English colonists didn't help to defend the Iroquois.

King Charles II sent soldiers to claim the territory of New York from the Dutch. The Dutch surrendered rather than fight English forces.

1664: The colony legalizes slavery.

1645   1650   1655   1660   1665   1670

March 12, 1664: King Charles II gives the Duke of York control over New York.

late 1660s: The English start trading with the Five Nations of the Iroquois.

The colony underwent several important changes during the late 1600s. On February 6, 1685, the Duke of York became King James II. This meant that New York became a royal colony. Then, in 1688, King James II made New York part of the Dominion of New England. Some colonists in New York distrusted England's power over this new, larger territory.

One of them was a German-born colonist named Jacob Leisler.

Leisler and his followers formed a small army. They took control of the colony's government in what became known as Leisler's Rebellion. But English soldiers arrested and executed Leisler in 1691.

New York faced another major challenge from the north. The French in Canada wanted to control parts of the colony. They teamed up with some of the area's American Indians. Together, they launched attacks on the English colonists during the 1700s.

King James II

1675–1676: A deadly war known as King Philip's War rages between colonists and American Indians. Colonists win the war with the help of the Five Nations.

1688: New York becomes part of the Dominion of New England.

1689: King James II ends the Dominion of New England.

1691: Leisler is arrested and killed.

1675   1680   1685   1690   1695   1700

mid-1670s: Colonists convince the Five Nations to fight with them against other American Indian tribes.

1685: The Duke of York becomes King James II. New York becomes a royal colony.

May 1689: Jacob Leisler and his followers take control of the colony's government.

The colony's growing slave population also created unrest. In 1712 about two dozen black slaves rebelled in New York City. They killed about ten white settlers. The settlers then arrested and executed twenty-one slaves. Despite these challenges, the colony continued to grow and thrive.

Jacob Leisler, here with his followers, seized control of New York in 1689 in Leisler's Rebellion. He was stopped two years later by the English.

1745: French troops and American Indian warriors begin attacks in New York.

1705   1710   1715   1735   1740   1745

1712: About two dozen black slaves rebel in New York City.

1741: New York has the largest slave population in the northern colonies.

New Jersey

Europeans first came to modern-day New Jersey in the early 1600s. The first settlers were from Finland, the Netherlands, and Sweden. In 1664 the Duke of York gave control of the land to two Englishmen. They were John Berkeley and George Carteret.

English settlers soon began arriving in what was then named the Province of New Jersey. French settlers also lived there. The population grew throughout the 1660s. By 1669 the colony had established its own legislature. Most of its elected lawmakers were colonists who had come from New England.

The lawmakers created religious conflict within the colony. They passed laws that limited voting rights. After that, only members of the Puritan church could vote. The governor disagreed with

COLONIAL GOVERNMENT

By the mid-1700s, most of the British colonies in America were royal colonies. The royal governor had the greatest power in each colony. He represented the desires of the king. At times, this caused conflict with the colonists. Some conflicts were over religious differences. Others had to do with issues of control, such as how businesses or farms should be run. To balance this power, most royal colonies elected their own legislature. The lawmakers worked with the governor to lead the colony.

1600   1610   1620   1660

early 1600s: Settlers from the Netherlands, Finland, and Sweden establish small settlements.

1664: The Duke of York gives New Jersey to John Berkeley and George Carteret.

these laws. He did not allow the legislature to meet again for seven years.

In 1674 Berkeley sold his claim over the colony to a group of Scottish investors. The investors took over the eastern half of the colony and called it East Jersey. The rest of the colony was known as West Jersey. By 1682 Carteret had sold West Jersey to some English investors. In 1702 the king united the two Jerseys into a single royal colony.

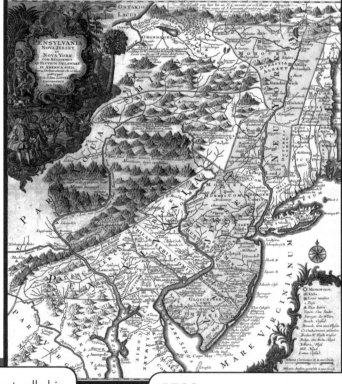

A map from 1756 shows Pennsylvania, New Jersey, New York, Connecticut, Massachusetts, and New Hampshire.

1674: Berkeley sells his claim to New Jersey.

1682: Carteret sells his claim to New Jersey.

1702: The colony's legislators pass laws making slavery legal.

1670   1680   1690   1700   1710

1675: New Jersey is divided in two.

1702: East Jersey and West Jersey are united and named New Jersey.

CHAPTER 5

The LAST ORIGINAL COLONIES

The histories of Delaware and Pennsylvania are connected. Both colonies belonged to William Penn. And both advanced the American ideals of religious freedom and tolerance. Along with Georgia, they were the last English colonies established in North America.

Delaware

Delaware started as a Dutch settlement in 1631. Eventually it became part of New Netherland. Like the rest of New Netherland, Delaware came under English control in 1664. eighteen years later, King Charles II granted the colony to William Penn. Penn was a wealthy Englishman who was also a Quaker. He controlled the neighboring land of Pennsylvania and put the two colonies together under one government.

The settlers in Delaware and Pennsylvania did not get along. Delaware colonists wanted to create an army. They

1636: Slaves are brought into Delaware.

1631: In April the Dutch establish a settlement in what became New Jersey.

1655: The Dutch take control of New Sweden, making it part of New Netherland.

DELAWARE

1630   1635   1640   1655   1660   1665   1670

1638: Swedish settlers arrive in March and name the land New Sweden.

1664: England takes control of New Netherland.

wished to protect their shores from French and pirate attacks. The Quakers of Pennsylvania did not believe in fighting wars. They did not support the idea of paying for an army.

In 1701 Penn agreed to create two separate colonies. Each would have its own legislature, but both would share one appointed governor. Delaware remained a small colony. With only thirty-three thousand residents by the mid-1700s, it was the smallest of all the colonies.

A wood engraving from 1882 shows William Penn arriving in New Castle, Delaware, in 1682.

1704: Colonists begin electing their own lawmakers.

1675   1680   1685   1690   1695   1700   1705

1682: King Charles II gives William Penn Delaware. Penn joins this new land with Pennsylvania.

1701: Penn agrees to separate Delaware from Pennsylvania.

Pennsylvania

Before gaining control of Delaware, William Penn established Pennsylvania. He and other Quakers wanted their own colony in the New World. In England they were punished for practicing their religion. King Charles II owed Penn's father money. In 1680 the king agreed to give William Penn a large amount of land in America. Royal officials called the colony Pennsylvania, or "Penn's Wood."

Penn valued the Quaker belief of tolerance. His colony allowed people to practice their own religions freely. He also lived by the Quaker values of fairness and honesty. That affected his dealings with local American Indians, such as the Lenni Lenape and Susquehannock.

Penn did not try to steal American Indian land. Instead, he established treaties. These treaties would allow colonists to settle on the land. But they also gave the American Indian communities the same rights that the settlers had. As a result, settlers had good relationships with the local tribes.

Penn also wanted to give colonists

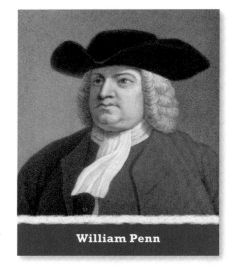

William Penn

1680: King Charles II grants William Penn Pennsylvania.

1682: Penn founds Philadelphia, the colony's new capital.

1680   **1682**   **1684**   **1686**   **1688**

1682: Penn arrives in Pennsylvania. He makes plans for a government of seventy-two elected men. The first Pennsylvania Council of elected men meets on December 4.

1688: A group of Quakers declare that slavery is against their Christian beliefs.

a real say in how Pennsylvania was governed. In 1682 he established a governing council of seventy-two men. These council members were elected by the free white men in the colony. The council then created the Great Law. The Great Law said members of all religions were equal and could vote. But only Christians could serve in government. The colony also welcomed people from different countries. In the 1680s, settlers came from Holland, Ireland, Wales, and Germany.

William Penn signs a treaty with the American Indians of the Pennsylvania region in 1683. This painting is by Benjamin West.

1692: King William III appoints a military governor named Captain Benjamin Fletcher.

late 1600s: American Indian tribes become trading partners with the colonists.

1690　　1692　　1694　　1696　　1698　　1700

1691: King William III makes Pennsylvania a royal colony.

1692–1694: Quaker representatives in the colony's assembly block Fletcher's efforts to lead.

1694: William III restores Penn's charter.

Changes soon came to Pennsylvania. The new king, William III, did not agree with Penn's ideas. In 1691 he took away Penn's charter and made Pennsylvania a royal colony. He also appointed a military officer as governor. The colony's Quakers did not support the king's action. They refused to support the new governor. The king gave in to the Quakers and restored Penn's charter in 1694.

The colony underwent more changes after Penn died in 1718. Settlers began taking land that belonged to American Indians. Some American Indian tribes fought back with attacks. In response, white settlers destroyed American Indian villages.

The colony grew quickly after 1720, as settlers from Germany, Switzerland,

QUAKERS IN THE NEW WORLD

From the start, religion was very important in Pennsylvania. But many Quaker beliefs were different from those of the Puritan and the Anglican colonists. For example, Quakers did not believe in paying taxes or fighting in wars. They also believed others should be free to practice their religions. Penn wanted his new colony to follow these beliefs. He called his colony a "holy experiment," an "example to the Nations," and a "free colony" where everyone was welcome.

1702   1704   1706   1708   1710

1701: Pennsylvania's elected lawmakers create the colony's fourth constitution. It divides the government into three separate branches: legislative, judicial, and executive.

and Scotland arrived. Pennsylvania became the third-largest colony, with more than 180,000 residents. Only Massachusetts and Virginia were bigger.

A historic illustration from around 1700 shows the Market House in downtown Philadelphia.

1732: Pennsylvanian Benjamin Franklin begins to publish *Poor Richard's Almanack.* It is one of a growing number of almanacs and newspapers printed in the colonies.

1718: William Penn dies.

1718   1720   1730   1740

1720s: More settlers arrive in Pennsylvania and settle on land owned by the Lenni Lenape without paying them for it.

1737: William Penn's son, Thomas Penn, tricks Delaware American Indians into giving up land in a deal known as the Walking Purchase.

Georgia

Georgia's beginnings were unique among the colonies. In the early 1730s, a group of wealthy Englishmen became interested in the territory. They called themselves the Georgia Trustees and were led by a man named James Oglethorpe.

The Georgia Trustees wanted to send poor English people to Georgia. It would be a fresh start for them. King George II and his government liked the idea. Georgia became the only American colony that Great Britain paid to help create.

Georgia was also unique because it was the only colony to ban slavery. Slavery made the creation of large plantations possible. But the Georgia Trustees did not want the colonists to spread out on large plantations. They wanted colonists to guard the border with Spanish Florida. That way, Georgia's people could defend the southern colonies against enemy attacks.

In addition, the trustees did not give the settlers any political power. Colonists could not elect their own lawmakers. Instead, the trustees appointed four officials to govern the colony.

James Oglethorpe

1732: The Georgia Trustees forbid slavery.

1733: Oglethorpe establishes the town of Savannah.

1734: Oglethorpe travels to England with Creek American Indians, who encourage all American Indians to make friendship treaties with the powerful British.

1730   1732   1734   1736   1738   1740

1732: King George II grants Georgia to the Georgia Trustees.

1733: James Oglethorpe brings settlers from England to Georgia.

1735: Colonists ask British authorities to legalize slavery.

GEORGIA

The colonists disliked these restrictions and protested against them. In the late 1730s, the trustees started to give the colonists more control. Slavery became legal in 1751. Soon after, the trustees turned Georgia over to the king. That made Georgia a royal colony with an elected legislature. Soon Georgia was like its neighbor, South Carolina. Wealthy white colonists owned large plantations. And they relied on a growing number of slaves.

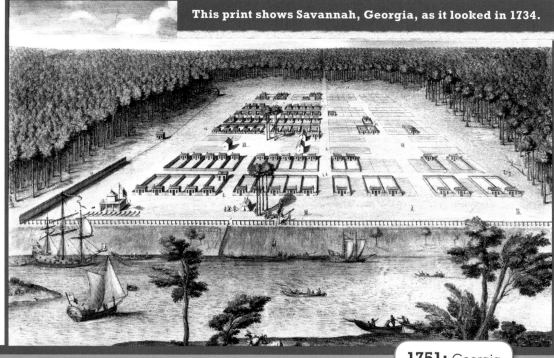

This print shows Savannah, Georgia, as it looked in 1734.

1751: Georgia Trustees allow slavery.

1742   1744   1746   1748   1750   1752

1742: Spanish troops attack Georgia, but Oglethorpe's troops drive them out in the Battle of Bloody Marsh.

1752: Georgia becomes a royal colony on July 4.

The Thirteen Colonies

By the mid-1700s, English settlers had formed the original thirteen colonies. Each of these colonies was established under different circumstances. And each colony attracted different kinds of settlers seeking different things from the New World. Yet, as they built the colonies together, the colonists came to see themselves not as settlers but as Americans.

The early colonists established the ideas that would eventually be the founding principles of the United States. From the earliest days, many colonists supported the idea of self-government. They wanted to elect the leaders who governed them. Later, some colonists promoted the principles

George Washington *(on white horse)* and a wounded General Edward Braddock appear in this 1854 painting of a battle scene during the French and Indian War.

1760s–1770s: Colonists protest new taxes imposed by the king and British lawmakers.

1754–1763: Colonists fight alongside British soldiers in a conflict known as the French and Indian War.

Fall 1774: Leaders from the colonies meet at the First Continental Congress to plan a response to British taxes.

1750   1755   1760   1765   1770

of no taxation without representation, freedom of religion, and the separation of church and state.

These ideas were not found everywhere in America. Yet they affected the way many colonists saw themselves. In each colony, people believed in their right to determine their own futures. The colonists' shared values and experiences united them. They also set the stage for the fight against British rule that would lead to the Revolutionary War.

Colonists in Massachusetts protest a taxation on tea by the British government during the Boston Tea Party in 1773.

April 19, 1775: The Battle of Lexington and Concord in Massachusetts marks the start of the Revolutionary War.

July 4, 1776: The Declaration of Independence announces the colonies' decision to separate from Great Britain.

1788: The United States adopts the US Constitution on June 21.

1775   1780   1785   1790   1795

May 1775: The Second Continental Congress meets in Philadelphia.

1781: The Battle of Yorktown in Virginia leads to a final American victory in the Revolutionary War.

1783: In September the Treaty of Paris between Great Britain and the United States marks the end of the Revolutionary War.

Writing Activity

Choose an event from one of the colony's timelines that interests you. Imagine you are a colonist who saw or participated in the event. Write a letter to someone back home describing what happened. Before writing, ask yourself these questions:

When did the event take place?

Where did it occur?

What did you see?

What did you do?

How did you feel?

Who was with you at the event?

What happened after the event?

How did the event change your future?

1732: The Georgia Trustees forbid slavery.

1692: Maryland becomes a royal colony.

1712: About two dozen black slaves rebel in New York City.

late 1600s: American Indian tribes become trading partners with the colonists.

1636: Slaves are brought into Delaware.

1637: The Pequot War ends after the English kill around 40 percent of the Pequots' two thousand men, women, and children.

1676: Nathaniel Bacon leads Bacon's Rebellion with the goal of killing every American Indian in Virginia.

1732: Benjamin Franklin begins to publish *Poor Richard's Almanack*. It is one of a growing number of almanacs and newspapers printed in the colonies.

1675: New Jersey is divided in two.

Glossary

Anglican: a member of the Church of England

appoint: to choose someone for a job or a task

colonize: to move into a new place and take over the land

convict: someone who has been found guilty of a crime

investor: someone who shares the cost and risk of a company or undertaking but also shares in the profits or rewards that are produced

legislature: an organized group of people who have the authority to make laws

merchant: a person who buys and sells goods

plantation: a large farm

tolerance: the acceptance of different beliefs and ideas

treaty: a written agreement

LERNER

SOURCE

Expand learning beyond the printed book. Download free, complementary educational resources for this book from our website, www.lernerresource.com.

Further Information

America's Story
http://www.americaslibrary.gov/jb/colonial/jb_colonial_subj.html
Explore the facts about colonial America at this Library of Congress website.

Archiving Early America
http://www.earlyamerica.com
Dive into more details about the nation's early years.

Figley, Marty Rhodes. *Who Was William Penn? And Other Questions about the Founding of Pennsylvania*. Minneapolis: Lerner Publications, 2012. Learn more about the founder of two of the original thirteen colonies.

Hamen, Susan E. *The Thirteen Colonies*. Minneapolis: Abdo Publishing, 2013. This fact-filled book describes how the colonies united against England.

History: Native Americans
http://video.nationalgeographic.com/video/kids/history-kids/native-americans-kids
Find out about America's original settlers, the American Indians.

Richards, Elizabeth. *The Founding of a Nation: The Story of the 13 Colonies*. Mustang, OK: Tate Publishing & Enterprises, 2008. Discover what life was really like in the colonies.

The Terrible Transformation: Africans in America
http://www.pbs.org/wgbh/aia/part1/narrative.html
Learn more about how African slaves fit into the history of America.

Waxman, Laura Hamilton. *Why Did the Pilgrims Come to the New World? And Other Questions about the Plymouth Colony*. Minneapolis: Lerner Publications, 2011. Explore the experience of the Pilgrims in more depth.

Index

Photo Acknowledgments

The images in this book are used with the permission of: © Ken Pilon/ Dreamstime.com, pp. 4–5; Courtesy National Park Service, Colonial National Historical Park, pp. 6–7; © The Bridgeman Art Library, pp. 8, 21, 25, 26; Wikimedia Commons, pp. 9, 12, 33; © Image Asset Management Ltd./SuperStock, p. 11; © North Wind Picture Archives, pp. 14, 23; © H -D Falkenstein/ima/imagebroker.net/SuperStock, pp. 15, 39; © Lee Snider/ Dreamstime.com, p. 17; © Peter Essick/Aurora/Getty Images, pp. 18-19; © SuperStock, p. 20; © James Lemass/SuperStock, p. 22; Library of Congress LC-USZ62-10293, p. 27; Library of Congress LC-USZC4-12217, p. 29; © National Portrait Gallery, London/The Bridgeman Art Library, p. 30; The Granger Collection, New York, pp. 31, 35, 41; © Stock Montage/Archive Photos/Getty Images, pp. 36, 40; Courtesy National Gallery of Art, Washington, p. 37; Library of Congress LC-USZC2-1689, p. 42; Courtesy Everett Collection, p. 43.

Front Cover: Library of Congress g3700 ar075700.

Main text font set in Caecilia Com 55 Roman 11/16.
Typeface provided by Linotype AG.